The Green Office
Boosting Sustainability and Efficiency at Work

Table of Contents

Chapter 1. Introduction

In this special report aptly titled, "The Green Office: Boosting Sustainability and Efficiency at Work," the world of business meets conscious, eco-friendly practices in an exciting, symbiotic harmony. This is no overly technical, heavy reading. Oh, no! It's an invigorating, hopeful look at how we can transform our workplaces into greener, more sustainable spaces — merely by making smart, mindful choices! Packed with actionable strategies and inspiring case studies, this report promises not only to enlighten you on the potential of green offices but also to arm you with the tools needed to implement such change. So, if you're teetering on the edge of a greener tomorrow, let this special report be the nudge that propels you forward! Come on, make the shift today. Your contribution can make a difference, and this report is the perfect place to start!

Chapter 2. The Green Pledge: Understanding Corporate Sustainability

To journey towards a greener tomorrow, our first step must be to understand and appreciate the concept of corporate sustainability. A mutually benefiting correlation, Corporate Sustainability focuses on balancing the responsibilities towards stakeholders, the environment, and most importantly, future generations.

2.1. A Closer Look into Corporate Sustainability

Corporate Sustainability is a business approach aimed at creating long-term stakeholder value through the implementation of a business strategy that focuses on the ethical, social, environmental, cultural, and economic dimensions of doing business. The strategies created are intended to foster longevity, transparency, and proper employee development within business organizations.

The manoeuvres don't stop at policy-making alone. They translate into everyday practices, decisions and company cultures to minimize the environmental footprint. Any organization practicing Corporate Sustainability is continuously making efforts to improve its operations and strive for excellence in environmental, social, and financial performance.

It's like taking a green pledge - a commitment that each member of your organization will develop and promote sustainable practices that reduce harm to the environment while still providing value to customers and stakeholders.

2.2. Corporate Sustainability: In Terms of Environmental Responsibility

Just as your body is a temple, so too is our Earth. Our actions must respect and protect the environment. Environmental responsibility in Corporate Sustainability refers to the duty that organizations have to minimize their environmental footprint. This is achieved by reducing resource consumption (water, energy, and raw materials), minimizing waste and emissions, and promoting recycling and use of renewable resources within the organization.

Notable measures include investing in energy-efficient technologies, transitioning to renewable energy sources, promoting reuse and recycling, and conducting regular environmental risk and impact assessments. Some businesses have gone as far as encouraging eco-friendly commuting among their staff and promoting the efficient use of utilities in their workplaces.

One inspiring case study is Patagonia, a well-known outdoor clothing brand. Patagonia has not only committed itself to build durable products, reducing the overall need for replacement but has also implemented initiatives like repairing and recycling clothing items, minimizing the demand for new clothing production and hence reducing its environmental footprint.

2.3. Corporate Sustainability: With Social Responsibility at Its Heart

Another pillar of Corporate Sustainability is Social Responsibility - demonstrating respect and concern for all stakeholders, be it employees, customers, or the communities in which businesses operate. Practices under this umbrella include providing a safe and encouraging work environment, promoting diversity and inclusiveness, offering fair wages and benefits, and engaging in community activities.

Starbucks, for instance, actively works towards ensuring fair trade practices. It creates employment opportunities in the communities it functions, sources products ethically and provides comprehensive employee benefits. All these endeavours make it an excellent example of social responsibility within corporate sustainability.

2.4. Economically Underpinning Corporate Sustainability

The train of Corporate Sustainability runs on the economic railtrack. In other words, a sustainable company must also be economically viable. Sustainability doesn't translate into bleeding resources-- financial or otherwise. Instead, it strives to balance profitability along with its social and environmental targets.

Creating value for shareholders while doing good for society and environment is a challenging task. However, businesses that succeed in doing so often reap rich rewards, including a positive corporate image, product differentiation, consumer goodwill, and increased profitability in the long term.

Unilever, for instance, through its Sustainable Living Plan, aims to double its revenue while reducing its overall environmental footprint and increasing its positive social impact. This practice has not only bolstered its market standing but also enhanced its brand value.

2.5. Looking into the Future: The Prospect of Corporate Sustainability

Replete with challenges as it might be, corporate sustainability holds a promising future. It's been universally accepted that companies operating sustainably are more likely to win over customers, attract and retain top talent, and achieve long-term shareholder value.

The road to corporate sustainability entails not just incorporating best practices into one's business model, but also actively innovating and adapting to the shifting business landscapes fostered by evolving technological, environmental and social conditions.

2.6. Crafting Your Corporate Sustainability Strategy

In order to develop a well-devised corporate sustainability strategy, an organization should focus on a long-term, panoramic vision which embraces green practices and encourages balance between meeting financial targets and enhancing the social and environmental aspects. This means gaining a clear understanding of stakeholders' needs and expectations and integrating sustainability into each individual's role in the organization.

In conclusion, to create a future where businesses thrive along with the environment and society, corporate sustainability is an indispensable approach. Understanding and implementing it would genuinely signify taking 'The Green Pledge.' The change starts with comprehension and is sustained by consistent, comprehensive actions. With this guide, you are equipped to make that change and lead your organization on the path of sustainability. By doing so, you become a part of the solution and foster a culture that values shared prosperity over isolated gain.

Chapter 3. Dissecting the Green Office: A Primer

Before we embark on this green journey, it's important to understand the concept of a green office, its core principles, and its components.

3.1. Conceptualizing The Green Office

The 'green office' moniker encompasses more than just the color. Rather, it refers to a workspace where attention to energy use, material consumption, and waste management takes precedence. A green office operates in a way that is beneficial both to the environment and the employees, noting that these two entities are, in fact, interdependent.

A green office employs strategies to reduce waste and energy consumption, enhance indoor air quality, create a healthier environment for employees, and, ultimately, contribute to saving our planet. It's a holistic approach that fuses environmental consciousness with a practical view to enhancing the user experience.

3.2. The Green Office: Core Principles

A green office operates on several core principles. These principles act as the driving force behind every decision.

- *Efficiency:* A green office places emphasis on energy-efficient appliances and processes.

- *Sustainability:* It prioritizes operating methods that don't deplete natural resources.

- *Health and wellness:* Enhanced employee wellbeing and productivity is a crucial component of a green office.

- *Waste reduction:* Green offices strive to minimize waste through recycling and healthy procurement strategies.

3.3. Components of A Green Office

There are specific elements that define a green office. These components must align perfectly to create an office that is truly green, and they range from the large, noticeable features down to the small, seemingly insignificant details.

3.3.1. The Building

Green offices prioritize energy-efficient buildings that leverage natural sunlight, utilize renewable energy sources, and have insulation to regulate temperature. The design of the building also plays a role, with green offices generally having more open spaces, indoor plants, and other biophilic elements.

3.3.2. Office Equipment and Supplies

Green offices prefer energy-efficient equipment and appliances. This extends to using LED light bulbs, energy star rated appliances, and energy-efficient HVAC systems. They also focus on sustainable procurement strategies to ensure office supplies are eco-friendly.

3.3.3. Waste Management

Catering to the principle of reducing waste, green offices incorporate conscientious waste management systems. This includes promoting recycling, composting organic waste, and electronics waste management.

3.3.4. Indoor Air Quality

Zeroing in on the wellbeing of employees, green offices pay close attention to maintaining a high indoor air quality, minimizing exposure to harmful chemicals. They prioritize indoor plants, which act as natural air purifiers, and use low VOC (volatile organic compounds) paints and furniture.

3.3.5. Transportation

Green offices also make it easier for their employees to choose eco-friendly commuting options. They provide bike storage, promote public transportation, or facilitate carpools.

3.3.6. Employee Education and Involvement

A green office isn't just built; it's nurtured every day by conscious decisions and actions of employees who've been educated about sustainability and actively participate in making greener choices.

As evident, the green office concept is broad, involving many different layers. These layers work interdependently towards a shared goal of reducing the environmental footprint. Through this chapter, we have lightly scratched the surface of each layer. In the upcoming segments, we will dive deeper, elaborating practical steps and strategies to creating each component of a green office.

Ready to pave the way for a greener future with us? Let's take this journey together, one where our actions result in a healthier planet and workforce! It's now time to delve deeper into the strategies that will help you materialize this vision. Let's swing open the door to our green office!

Chapter 4. Designing for Efficiency: Sustainable Office Layouts

In today's world, striving for sustainability is far from new, but when it comes to office design, it tends to be eclipsed by aesthetics or immediate practicality. However, embracing sustainable office layouts can change the overall environment, induce productivity, increase energy efficiency, and reduce carbon footprints. As we unveil the steps and strategies to design green offices, we'll show examples and reveal the immense potential of this venture.

4.1. The Eco-Friendly Layout Foundation

Sustainable office design starts with the basics: the layout. An eco-friendly layout can enhance natural light, improve air quality, reduce energy consumption, and promote a healthier, more productive workflow.

Incorporate as much natural light as possible. Redesign office spaces to decrease dependence on artificial light sources. If possible, offer everyone a window view. Not only does natural light reduce electricity usage, but it also boosts mood and productivity, and decreases the risk of eyestrain.

Air quality is another primary concern. An office layout that promotes proper ventilation can improve air quality and reduce reliance on air conditioning. Cooler work environments contribute to increased productivity and improve health, reducing sick days.

Moreover, a thoughtful layout can help manage noise pollution and control acoustics, mitigating distractions and enhancing productivity. Noise control is often overlooked in office design, but it's essential for fostering an effective workplace.

4.2. Going for Green Building Materials

When designing your office layout, consider the materials used for construction and furnishings. Choosing sustainable materials can significantly cut down on your office's environmental impact.

You can opt for construction materials with lower "embodied energy" - the total energy used in the production process. Reclaimed, recycled and local materials often have a lower embodied energy and hence are more sustainable.

For interiors, consider furnishings made from reclaimed materials. Additionally, seek out low-impact materials, which do not emit harmful Toxic Organic Compounds (TOCs). These compounds can contribute to 'sick building syndrome,' causing headaches and other health issues in employees.

Another strategy is using modular furniture that can be easily reconfigured, minimizing waste when company needs change. Furthermore, think about furniture lifecycle management, ideally purchasing items that are durable, repairable, and ultimately recyclable.

4.3. Opting for Energy-Efficient Appliances

Your office will need appliances, equipment, and gadgets. Choose energy-efficient models wherever possible. An ENERGY STAR rating, for example, signifies equipment designed to save energy without compromising functionality.

Computers, printers, copy machines, fridges - there are ENERGY STAR alternatives for all these essential office tools. The saved energy can equate to lower operational costs and a smaller carbon footprint. It's worth researching the most energy-efficient models, even if they might cost more upfront.

Remember to consider the lifecycle cost of each product - not just the initial price but long-term energy usage, maintenance, and eventual disposal.

4.4. The Power of Plants

Indoor plants offer a multitude of benefits. They improve air quality by absorbing CO_2 and releasing oxygen. Through this process, they also absorb harmful toxins and increase humidity, which can help reduce air conditioning use.

Adding greenery can also boost staff morale and productivity. Studies link interaction with nature to lower stress levels, increased feelings of wellbeing, and improved cognitive function.

Therefore, a sustainable office layout isn't complete without a few plants. Low-maintenance species like snake plants, peace lilies, and bamboo palms can work exceptionally well in office environments.

4.5. Space Utilization

Not every company can afford a sprawling, open floor office layout. However, a small workspace doesn't have to impede sustainability goals. With careful planning and innovative design, you can create a green, efficient layout in a more confined space.

Consider things like flexible seating options, mobile furniture, and multi-purpose rooms. Deployment of such strategies helps to optimize the use of space, which indirectly contributes to sustainability by reducing the need for bigger properties and the associated energy costs.

4.6. Implementing Technology for Sustainability

To create a sustainable office layout, you don't have to rely solely on architecture and design elements. Incorporating technology can play a vital role too.

Consider implementing a Building Management System (BMS). These systems allow for advanced control over energy use, adjusting heating, cooling, and lighting based on the need. Many BMS can be controlled remotely, making them an excellent solution for reducing energy consumption outside of office hours.

In conclusion, sustainability in office layouts is more than just a buzzword. It is a design philosophy that has outstanding implications on both an organization's bottom line and its environmental impact. By incorporating an efficient, eco-friendly layout, leveraging green materials, choosing energy-efficient appliances, using greenery, optimizing space, and implementing suitable technology, we can all contribute to a greener, more sustainable working world.

Chapter 5. Energy Conservation Measures at Work

Green offices start with an astute focus on energy conservation. It's the first, significant step toward a sustainable, eco-friendly working environment. Through energy conservation methods, businesses can reduce their carbon footprint, cut down costs, and create better workplaces.

5.1. Understanding Your Energy Profiles

The first step in conserving energy at work is understanding your energy profiles. Energy profiling entails recording and analyzing energy consumption patterns over some time. In office settings, this can imply studying how power is used across various elements, from lighting and heating to computer use and air conditioning.

Several energy monitoring tools available on the market can assist with this, offering the functionality to track energy usage, define trends and patterns, and even identify anomalies or points of excessive power use.

5.2. Office Equipment and Energy-Saving Practices

Office equipment can be a major energy drain. Computers, printers, photocopiers, and even the coffee maker contribute to your energy usage profile.

A few energy-saving practices can drastically reduce energy consumption:

- **Turn it off:** Instruct employees to switch off their computers, monitors, and other office equipment when not in use.

- **Implement power-saving modes:** Many electrical devices have power-saving features that reduce energy usage during periods of inactivity.

- **Opt for energy-efficient products:** When purchasing new equipment, consider energy efficiency ratings. These can regularly use less energy and contribute to long-term energy-saving efforts.

5.3. Lighting: Lowering Energy Consumption

Lighting is another chief contributor to energy usage in an office. Illuminating your space efficiently could lead to significant energy savings.

- **Maximize Natural Light:** Use natural light to your advantage. Arrange interiors to benefit from natural light, such as keeping workstations near windows.

- **Switch to Energy-Efficient Bulbs:** Energy-saving light bulbs, like LED and CFL, use far less energy than traditional incandescent bulbs, and they last longer.

- **Install Motion Sensor Lighting:** Motion sensor lights in areas used less frequently can prevent unnecessary energy consumption.

5.4. Better Building Insulation

Insulation is crucial to maintaining a comfortable temperature in an office, containing warm or cool air longer within, and reducing the need for excessive HVAC system usage. Effective insulation can significantly reduce heating and cooling costs.

Types of efficient insulations include blanket (batts and rolls), concrete block, foam board or rigid foam, insulating concrete forms (ICFs), loose-fill and blown-in, and reflective system.

5.5. Heating, Ventilation, and Air Conditioning (HVAC) Systems

Heating, Ventilation, and Air conditioning (HVAC) systems account for approximately 44% of commercial buildings' energy consumption in the United States.

Several strategies can help a business conserve energy within the realm of HVAC:

- **Routine preventive maintenance**: Regular maintenance of the HVAC systems is the key to their efficient operation. Regular change of air filters, checking thermostats and controls, and other necessary maintenance are key.

- **Utilization of programmable thermostats**: Programmable thermostats offer substantial energy-saving potential. These can be set to adjust the temperature when the building or certain packets are unoccupied.

- **Upgrade systems to high-efficiency units**: A high-efficiency HVAC system generally uses less energy, helping in energy conservation.

5.6. The Role of Renewable Energy

Renewable energy solutions such as solar panels, wind power, or geothermal power can play an essential role in reducing a business's reliance on grid energy. They offer long-term energy conservation, decrease carbon emissions, and often save money.

Harnessing renewable energy could mean installing solar panels onto the building's rooftops or even purchasing green energy from providers. Such initiatives show corporate commitment to sustainability, often appealing to both employees and customers.

5.7. Encourage Employee Engagement

Beyond structural and technological energy conservation efforts, fostering an energy-saving culture within the organization is crucial to success. Engage employees in saving energy, offering education about energy conservation and encouraging responsible behaviors.

Conduct seminars, talk about energy-saving goals, introduce rewards for energy-saving efforts – create an engaging, positive, and responsible dialogue around energy conservation.

Incorporating energy conservation into work practices doesn't just benefit the business with reduced utility bills. It contributes to a more sustainable future, improves public image, and can even increase employee satisfaction. Remember, starting small can lead to big changes, and every effort counts in the grand scheme of energy conservation. There's no better time than now to start making those energy-conscious changes.

Chapter 6. Materials Matter: Choosing Eco-Friendly Office Supplies

The shift towards greener office supplies begins with a fundamental understanding of the materials we routinely use in our workplaces. For too long, businesses have overlooked the environmental impact of underlying materials utilized in standard office supplies. Plastics, processed wood, and chemicals found in everyday items from pens to post-it notes contribute significantly towards pollution and resource depletion. Transitioning to eco-friendly alternatives can reduce our carbon footprint and help preserve our planet.

6.1. Understanding the Environmental Impact of Standard Office Supplies

A vital starting point to transform office supplies is understanding their environmental impact. Most office supplies comprise materials that significantly contribute to our global environmental crisis. For instance, standard paper is usually derived from logging activities that play a part in deforestation. Plastics, commonly used in products like pens, computer keyboards, and staplers, are petroleum-based, non-biodegradable, and sometimes contain toxic chemicals harmful for human health and the environment.

Similarly, other office supplies like ink cartridges, electronics, and batteries contain heavy metals and noxious chemicals, which, when improperly discarded, leach into soil and water bodies, causing pollution and harming wildlife. Acknowledging the contribution of these materials to environmental harm helps motivate the shift towards greener alternatives.

6.2. Eco-Friendly Alternatives

Conscious choices about the materials we use can lead to significant environmental improvements. Options for eco-friendly materials and products are increasingly available, catering to a variety of office needs.

1. PAPER: Choose paper made from recycled materials, post-consumer waste, or sustainably sourced wood pulp. Some manufacturers have started producing tree-free paper from materials like bamboo, sugarcane, or hemp, which require less energy and water to process.

2. PENS & PENCILS: Look for pens and pencils made from recyclable materials, biodegradable plastics, or even reclaimed wood. Some pens are refillable, reducing the need for replacements and thereby lowering waste production.

3. NOTEBOOKS: Opt for notebooks made from recycled or tree-free paper. Several suppliers offer cover materials made from recycled cardboard or other low-impact materials.

4. OFFICE FURNITURE: Whenever possible, purchase second-hand furniture or furniture made from reclaimed or sustainable materials like bamboo, cork, or sustainably-harvested wood.

5. INK & TONER: Purchase remanufactured ink and toner cartridges. These products are assembled from recycled cartridges and are a much greener choice than buying new.

6.3. The Power of Procurement Policies

Implementing eco-friendly procurement policies can profoundly influence an organization's environmental impact. By preferring eco-friendly suppliers and materials, businesses can stimulate demand for sustainable products, bolstering their market presence and leading to better product development and lower prices. Consider working with suppliers who adhere to green standards, employ fair trade practices, and prioritize waste reduction and recycling. Such considerations might include looking for certifications like FSC for paper products or Energy Star for electronics.

6.4. Case Study: A Green Office Success Story

To illustrate the above points, let's consider a case study. ABC Corporation, a mid-sized tech firm, decided to switch to 100% eco-friendly office supplies. In the first year, the decision paid off immensely:

1. The company successfully reduced its paper consumption by 30% with a switch to digital processes and using recycled paper whenever physical copies were necessary.

2. Opting for refillable pens led to a substantial decrease in the volume of plastic waste produced.

3. Furniture purchases were made from vendors offering sustainable or pre-used products, minimizing the carbon footprint tied to producing new furniture.

4. ABC Corporation's green initiatives did not stop with materials. They also updated their procurement policies, preferring suppliers who showcased transparent and sustainable practices.

6.5. Conclusion: It's Easier Than You Think!

Transitioning to environmentally friendly office supplies and materials is not the daunting task it may first appear. It requires thoughtful choices and conscious consumption, beginning with an understanding of the environmental impact of standard supplies and making a commitment to change. From there, a plethora of alternatives and a decisive shift in procurement policies can inspire collective change that reduces our environmental footprint and paves the way for a greener, healthier planet.

Chapter 7. Workplace Wellness: The Health Benefits of Green Spaces

Integrating green spaces into our daily work environments can offer a staggering number of health and wellness benefits. With illnesses and stress often exacerbated due to unhealthy, sterile workplaces, the call for green offices has never been louder. We might not realize it, but the impact of our surroundings on our health and wellbeing is both profound and holistic.

7.1. The Science Behind Green Spaces and Wellness

The world of science has much to say about the health benefits of incorporating green areas into offices. It's no secret that nature has a soothing impact on human beings. Studies undertaken across different age groups and cultures consistently highlight that exposure to green spaces reduces stress levels and improves mood.

When incorporated into workplaces, this has far-reaching benefits. Stress reduction, enhanced mood, and improved cognitive function are just a few of the benefits that can boost employee wellness and productivity. Plus, these greener workplaces reduce exposure to air pollutants and offer employees a refreshing and peaceful environment in which they can work.

7.2. Biophilia and Biophilic Design

Derived from the Greek words for 'life' and 'love,' biophilia implies a natural propensity in humans to connect with nature and other forms of life. This innate connection we have with nature, as suggested by Harvard naturalist Dr. Edward O. Wilson, can significantly boost our health and well-being.

Biophilic design focusses on introducing aspects of nature into human-made environments. In offices, this could mean having plants, natural materials, and lighting, or even views of a landscaped area or access to a garden. Over the years, studies suggest that such environments enhance people's physical and mental health dramatically–even fostering creativity and attention.

7.3. Physical Health Benefits

A major aspect of workplace wellness is the physical health of employees. Green offices provide numerous benefits in this realm, too. Indoor plants have been found to purify the air by eliminating toxic agents. They act as natural air purifiers and oxygen generators.

Green offices can also reduce noise levels. Plants, trees, and even lawns inside an office can substantially dampen noise, contributing to a healthier and more focused environment.

Healthy indoor environments can result in fewer instances of 'sick building syndrome,' where occupants experience health issues and discomfort due to time spent in certain building conditions. Fewer health complaints mean fewer sick days and improved productivity.

7.4. Psychological Health Benefits

Increased greenery in the workplace not only aids physical health but also significantly improves psychological well-being. The psychological benefits of green spaces include stress reduction, increased relaxation, and improved mood.

Exposure to natural light aids office workers' mental well-being and alertness. Similarly, viewing natural landscapes and elements can reduce mental fatigue and improve focus and concentration.

Having access to green spaces can also encourage social interactions among employees, thereby fostering a sense of community and reducing feelings of isolation.

7.5. Case Studies

Let us now look at some inspiring real-world applications of these principles. The ANZ Centre in Melbourne, Australia, features a large, open atrium filled with plants, demonstrating biophilic design. On conducting a post-occupancy survey, ANZ found that this green office led to a 15% increase in staff perceptions of well-being.

In another case, the Human Spaces report involving 7600 workers from 16 countries, found that employees with access to nature reported 15% higher levels of overall well-being.

7.6. The Time to Act

The time has come to transition to healthier, happier workplaces. Workplace wellness is an investment that companies make in their most important resource – their employees. By integrating nature into office design, companies can reap benefits extending far beyond aesthetics, contributing significantly to employee health, productivity, and satisfaction.

To guide this shift, businesses can refer to resources such as the WELL Building Standard and the Living Building Challenge. These documents offer a wealth of information on achieving wellness through building design. A green office is not a distant dream, but a feasible, constructive reality that we can strive for today to ensure our collective well-being in the future.

In conclusion, the benefits of green spaces in workplaces extend from enhancing physical and psychological health to boosting social connections, productivity, and overall employee satisfaction. It's a win-win situation for employers and employees alike, and the sooner we embrace it, the better we are poised to thrive in a competitive market.

Chapter 8. Technology as an Ally: Innovative Tools for Sustainability

When we talk about sustainability in offices, technology is often seen as the problem. After all, devices like computers, lights, and air conditioning units are all notorious energy consumers. But what if we could turn the tables and use technology as an instrument for sustainability instead? This chapter provides an exhaustive and detailed look at innovative technologies that can aid us in our quest for greener offices.

8.1. The Internet of Things (IoT) for Energy Efficiency

A promising technology in this area is the Internet of Things (IoT). At a basic level, IoT refers to the interconnection of everyday devices via the internet, allowing them to send and receive data. In a green office, IoT could be used to monitor and control energy usage with smart sensors and devices.

Consider, for instance, a scenario where every device in an office is connected to an IoT framework. The IoT system could be set up so that devices are only on when they're needed. If there are no employees in a room, the lights and computer screens switch off automatically, and the heating or cooling adjusts accordingly reducing overall energy use.

8.2. Virtual "Green" Conferencing

Another area where technology can help usher in more sustainable business practices is by reducing the need for travel. Virtual meetings, powered by services like Zoom or Microsoft Teams, are not just a substitute for face-to-face meetings, they are often more efficient. They save time, resources, and eliminate the carbon emissions that would have been created from travel.

8.3. Green Data Centers

Data centers consume massive amounts of energy due to their need to be constantly operational and cooled. Green data centers, or eco-friendly data centers, aim to resolve this issue. They are designed to consume less energy and minimize environmental impact. They do this by using energy-efficient hardware, reducing dependency on air conditioning with natural cooling methods, and using renewable energy sources.

8.4. Cloud Computing

Similarly, moving to cloud services can also reduce carbon footprints. Instead of every company having its own servers, which use up substantial energy, businesses can now share server space located remotely. This tends to be more energy-efficient, as cloud providers are incentivized to minimize energy usage in their mega data centers to keep costs down.

8.5. Sustainable Web Design

Website energy consumption often flies under the radar in the conversation about green business practices, but it contributes significantly to digital carbon footprints. Efficient, uncluttered websites use less energy to load and run — a small but valuable step to making a business more sustainable.

8.6. Greening IT Equipment

Let's not forget the potential of greening the technology equipment we use daily. Energy Star rated office equipment, for instance, uses significantly less energy than standard office equipment. Also, considering lifecycle stages while purchasing equipment can contribute to sustainability. Equipment that is durable, upgradable, and recyclable helps to save energy and reduce waste.

8.7. Power Management Software

Investing in power management software is another strategy to ensure greener practices in the office. These tools manage the power usage of various devices within the office, scheduling when devices go into low-power (sleep) mode or shutting them down entirely during non-office hours.

8.8. Paperless Transactions

Finally, moving towards paperless transactions can significantly cut down on the demand for paper and the need for storage space. Electronic invoicing, document signing, and file sharing reduce paper usage while increasing efficiency.

As we have seen, technology doesn't have to be the enemy of sustainability. Instead, when strategically used, it can provide innovative solutions to help businesses become more energy-efficient and sustainable, leading to greener, smarter offices. It's all about making smart, mindful switches— and this journey begins with awareness. The only question left is this: are you ready to leverage technology for sustainability in your office?

Chapter 9. Case Studies: Green Office Success Stories Globally

Whether it's the bustling start-ups of Silicon Valley or the historical business titans of Europe, organizations across the world have been realizing the potential of sustainable office solutions. In this chapter, we'll explore some of the most inspiring success stories of green offices globally.

9.1. The Adobe Headquarters: Pioneer in Green Retrofitting

Let's start our journey on the west coast of the United States, in San Jose, California. Adobe's global headquarters, in a trio of skyscrapers housing over 4,000 employees, is a leading example of eco-friendly practices.

In 2002, Adobe undertook a substantial green retrofit of their towers. They deployed a set of 64 distinct energy conservation measures, including advanced light controls, upgraded HVAC systems, waterless urinals, and a green cleaning program. Remarkably, the initial investment of around $1.4 million was recouped within ten months, and since then, Adobe has continued to save approximately $1.2 million every year on utility costs alone.

Moreover, Adobe's actions had substantial environmental benefits. Their efforts led to a reduction of more than 121 million pounds of CO2 (an equivalent to taking 10,880 cars off the road for a year), and 78 million gallons of water saved - that's about 118 Olympic-sized swimming pools!

9.2. The Pearl River Tower: A Symbiosis of Architecture and Sustainability

Asia's shining beacon of sustainability is located in Guangzhou, China - the Pearl River Tower. Considered one of the most energy-efficient buildings globally, it is a majestic 71-story high rise that blends structural design with eco-friendly technology.

Designed by the renowned architectural firm Skidmore, Owings & Merrill, the tower's unique shape optimizes the use of wind power, thanks to wind turbines built directly into its architecture. The tower's other green features include radiant cooling ceiling panels, under-floor ventilation, solar panels, and a double skin facade that reduces heat absorption.

9.3. The Powerhouse Brattørkaia: A Positive Energy Space

In the chilly climes of Norway, we find the Powerhouse Brattørkaia, the world's northernmost energy-positive building. Located in the heart of Trondheim, this office building produces more than twice the energy it consumes, all through renewable sources.

The building's energy surplus heats surrounding buildings and electric vehicles through a local micro-grid. The key to its energy production lies in its 3,000-square meter solar cell-clad roof and facade. Its energy-efficient design, coupled with its waste heat capturing system, ensure minimal energy wastage.

9.4. The Bullitt Center: The Greenest Commercial Building

When it comes to marrying ecological responsibility with cutting-edge design, few can match the Bullitt Center in Seattle, USA. Often touted as the greenest commercial building in the world, the six-story, 50,000-square foot office space embodies the ideals of energy-efficiency and carbon neutrality.

The building earns its unique title through its extensive use of renewable energy, composting toilets, and a rainwater-to-potable-water system. With its impressive 575 solar panels, the roof generates nearly 230,000 kWh of electricity annually, enough to power 20 average American homes for a year.

9.5. Conclusion: A Global Green Trend

As showcased by these diverse yet equally inspiring case studies, the green office trend is not confined to a single region or culture. It's a remarkable testament to human ingenuity, adaptability, and an increasing sense of responsibility towards nurturing the planet. By learning from their experiences, we can fast track our journey towards a greener, healthier, and more sustainable future.

Chapter 10. Roadmap to Transformation: Implementing Green Practices

The journey towards a green office begins with commitment and a well-structured plan. Though the notion of introducing green practices to your workspaces may seem daunting, this transformation can be achieved in simple, practical steps. Implementing thoughtful planning, top-down commitment, and strategic investments can have a profound impact on your organization's sustainability efforts. This chapter outlines the roadmap to effectively implement eco-friendly and sustainable practices in your office environments.

10.1. Understanding Your Baseline

Some standard practices will have far-reaching effects on how green your office is, and the first step would be to understand where you are today. Before making changes, organizations should assess their current state and build a baseline. This includes the consumption of resources like energy, water, and raw materials, as well as the generation of waste and emissions.

Use energy monitoring systems to track the amount of electricity consumed during a specific period. Similarly, examine your water usage patterns, and consider utilizing water-efficient fixtures. Check your supply chain to identify the amount of raw materials consumed in your process and the subsequent waste output. This kind of thorough audit will provide you with a clear picture of your environmental footprint and can point out the areas where immediate improvement can be achieved.

10.2. Committing to Change

Once you understand where you stand, the next step is committing to make the necessary changes for a greener and sustainable future. This commitment must be made from the top-down, starting with leadership. Leaders set the tone and culture of an organization, and their commitment to supporting sustainability initiatives can motivate employees to adapt and pick up new practices that focus on environmental well-being. Engagement through regularly scheduled meetings, workshops, and training sessions can improve employee involvement in green initiatives and encourage everyone to make eco-friendly decisions in their daily routines.

10.3. Identifying Goals and Setting Targets

Green practices should be aligned to particular business objectives and sustainability goals. The goal setting process involves identifying critical areas for improvement and setting realistic and measurable targets. Clearly articulate what you hope to achieve by implementing green practices - this could involve reducing energy consumption by a specific percentage, achieving zero waste, or launching a comprehensive recycling program.

When setting sustainability goals, remember to keep them SMART - Specific, Measurable, Achievable, Relevant, Time-bound. Specific goals have a clear outcome, measurable goals can be tracked, achievable goals are within reach, relevant goals align with your organization's mission, and time-bound goals have a set timeline for completion.

10.4. Implementing Green Practices

With goals in place, the practicalities of implementing green office practices come into play. This phase dives into the heart of sustainable work environments, introducing changes that range from minor tweaks to larger, significant investments.

Small changes could include things like switching to LED lights, minimizing printing, encouraging reusable water bottles, and adjusting thermostat settings. Larger initiatives might involve installing solar panels, replacing old equipment with energy-efficient ones, or integrating green materials in building design and furniture.

Investments must also be made in training personnel who understand and can implement sustainable practices. Such training can be done in-house or through various sustainability programs and workshops.

10.5. Monitoring and Evaluation

To ensure the continued effectiveness of your green practices, implement a structured monitoring program that continuously measures performance against your set goals. Regular audits and reviews will help keep the initiatives on track.

This involves collecting data related to your targets - energy usage, water consumption, waste generation and how effectively it is managed, and the overall productivity of the office. Any anomalies from the set baseline should trigger a review and tweaking of the practices to align better with the objectives.

While this journey towards a greener, more sustainable office might seem daunting, keep in mind that every change, small or significant, counts. Remember that implementing these green practices not only benefits the environment but also impacts the office in ways that can improve efficiency, productivity, and overall health and morale of employees. Keep the dialogue alive, continue learning, and expand your efforts. The road to transformation may be long, but the rewards reaped are well worth it.

Chapter 11. Encouraging Participation: Involving Employees in the Green Movement

Effective environmental and green initiatives cannot be driven solely by executive decisions. They require involvement from everyone in the organization to trickle down sustainability principles effectively. This chapter delves into strategies that can encourage all employees to participate in the green movement actively.

11.1. Understanding the Importance

Firstly, educating employees about the significance of sustainability and the impact of their choices is crucial. Workshops, webinars, and interactive group sessions can accomplish this. Experts in the field of sustainability can be invited to shed light on the subject. These activities should emphasize how a culture of sustainability can benefit not just the environment, but also the company's bottom line and their work environment. Show examples of companies thriving due to their environmental policies, and stress on the dire consequences of unfettered usage of finite resources.

11.2. Green Teams

Creating a "Green Team" can fuel engagement. This group should ideally comprise members from different departments, so there's representation from all parts of the organization. An IT member might have excellent ideas concerning data centers and energy efficiency, while a human resources representative may provide insights about promoting a green culture throughout the company.

11.3. Rewards and Recognition

To incentivize participation, companies can establish a rewards system. Prizes can be offered to employees or departments that recycle the most, save the most energy, or come up with innovative sustainability ideas. This can make going green both fun and rewarding.

11.4. Suggestions and Feedback

Regular channels for suggestions and feedback should be established. This will allow employees an opportunity to voice their ideas and feel involved in the process of going green. These channels can be physical suggestion boxes, emails, or digital platforms.

11.5. Changes at Personal Workstations

Sustainability can also begin at an individual level. Encourage employees to minimize waste at their desks, reduce paper use, and use power-saving options on their computers. Work towards creating a digital-oriented culture that diminishes the dependency on paper.

11.6. Awareness Campaigns

Holding awareness campaigns also helps in embedding the culture of sustainability within an organization. Such campaigns can serve to highlight earth-friendly ways to travel to work, the benefits of buying second-hand items, the importance of turning off lights and computers, and energy-efficient practices.

11.7. Workplace Infrastructure Changes

Green initiatives also need to be reflected in the workplace infrastructure. Adopting open offices that allow natural light, using ergonomic furniture that's both comfortable and environmentally friendly, automatic lights that save energy, and waste segregation are some of the changes that can be made.

11.8. Training Programs

In addition to awareness, it is also essential to provide employees with the necessary training on how to implement green practices at their work. This can range from correct recycling practices, energy-saving measures, or even programs about adopting green practices in their lives outside of work.

11.9. Employee Benefits that Encourage Sustainability

Providing benefits that promote sustainability, such as discounts for employees who buy hybrid vehicles or use public transportation, can also stimulate employee involvement. Such practices not only promote a green culture but also save costs in the long run by reducing energy consumption and waste.

11.10. Collaboration with External Green Initiatives

Companies can also collaborate with external green initiatives to lead by example. For instance, initiatives to clean local neighborhoods, tree planting drives, and collaborations with local communities to build green spaces can be participated in.

By involving all employees in the process of going green, we can promote a sense of unity and collaboration. Remember, the journey to sustainability does not end after implementing these plans; it's only the beginning of an ongoing, rewarding endeavor that benefits the company, its employees, and most importantly—the planet.